WHAT ARE THE BOOKS OF NAHUM–MALACHI?

Kids' Guides to God's Word Series

What Are the Books of NAHUM–MALACHI?

Michael Whitworth

ISBN 978-1-971767-28-4

Published by Start2Finish
Bend, Oregon 97702
start2finish.org

Printed in the United States of America
30 29 28 27 26   1 2 3 4 5

CONTENTS

INTRODUCTION

The previous volume of this series ended with the prophet Micah standing in the foothills of Judah, looking up at a corrupt Jerusalem and asking one of the most beautiful questions in the Bible: "Who is a God like you, who pardons sin and forgives the transgression of the remnant of his inheritance?"

Then he answered his own question. God hurls our sins into the depths of the sea. He delights to show mercy. His faithfulness outlasts our failure, every single time.

That was the last word of Micah. But it wasn't the last word of the Minor Prophets.

Six voices remain. And they will carry us through the most dramatic centuries in Old Testament history—from the fall of the mightiest empire the ancient world had ever seen to the rebuilding of a ruined temple, from the depths of exile to the fragile hope of return, and finally to the edge of a four-hundred-year silence that would only be broken by an angel appearing to a priest and a baby crying in a manger.

These six prophets are the bridge between the Old Testament and the New. Skip them, and you'll arrive at the Gospels without understanding how the story got there. Read them, and you'll discover that every thread the Bible has been weaving since Genesis comes together in these small, fierce, extraordinary books.

WHERE WE ARE IN THE STORY

The previous volume covered Hosea, Joel, Amos, Obadiah, Jonah, and Micah. Most of those prophets preached during the eighth century BC, when both Israel and Judah were still standing but rotting from the inside. They warned of coming judgment. They pleaded for repentance. And they pointed, even through the darkness, toward a God whose mercy would outlast every failure.

By the time our story picks up in Nahum, some of those warnings have come true. The northern kingdom of Israel fell to Assyria in 722 BC and never recovered. The ten northern tribes were scattered and absorbed into the nations. Only the southern kingdom, Judah, remained, clinging to Jerusalem and the temple and the promises of God.

But Judah's survival was precarious. For over a century, they lived under the shadow of the Assyrian Empire, paying tribute, compromising their worship, and wondering if God still cared. Then Assyria itself began to crumble. Babylon rose to take its place. And in 586 BC, the unthinkable happened: Babylon destroyed Jerusalem, burned the temple to the ground, and dragged God's people into exile.

The exile lasted roughly seventy years. When a remnant finally returned under Persian rule, they found a ruined city, an empty temple site, and a future that looked nothing like the glorious restoration the prophets had promised. They rebuilt slowly, struggled constantly, and waited for a God who sometimes seemed painfully silent.

That's the world of these final six prophets. They span about two hundred years of history, from the last days of Assyrian dominance to the quiet decades after the return from exile. And together, they tell a story that moves from judgment to hope, from destruction to rebuilding, and from waiting to the edge of fulfillment.

WHAT YOU'RE ABOUT TO READ

Each of these prophets has a distinct voice and a distinct moment, but they're all part of the same story.

Nahum is the prophet of Assyria's destruction. For over a century, the Assyrian Empire had terrorized the ancient world with a cruelty that defies description. Nahum announces that God has seen every atrocity, and that the empire everyone thought was untouchable is about to be erased from the earth. His message is terrifying to the oppressor and deeply comforting to the oppressed.

Habakkuk is the prophet who argued with God. Instead of delivering God's message to the people, Habakkuk delivered the people's questions to God. Why does evil go unpunished? Why would God use a wicked nation to judge a less wicked one? The answers he received didn't make things easier, but they produced one of the most important sentences in the Bible: "The righteous will live by faith."

Zephaniah is the prophet of the day of the Lord. His vision of coming judgment sweeps from Jerusalem to the ends of the earth, describing a day so overwhelming that language itself buckles under the weight. But the book that begins with un-creation ends with God singing over his people in joy. The contrast is staggering.

Haggai is the prophet who got things done. After the return from exile, the people rebuilt their own houses but left God's temple in ruins for eighteen years. Haggai's blunt, practical message shamed them into action, and within weeks the work had begun. His book is the shortest and most precisely dated in the Old Testament, and it proves that prophets aren't just preachers. Sometimes they're project managers.

Zechariah is the prophet of visions and the coming King. His book is the longest of the Minor Prophets and the most frequently quoted in the Gospel accounts of Jesus' death. In the first half, eight bizarre and beautiful night visions reveal what God is doing behind the scenes. In the second half, prophecies describe a coming king who rides a donkey, is valued at thirty pieces of silver, is pierced by his own people, and is struck down by God's own design. No book in the Old Testament points more directly at the cross.

Malachi is the last voice before the silence. Preaching to a tired, cynical nation that has stopped caring about God, Malachi confronts their apathy with devastating honesty. But his book ends not with judgment but with a promise: the sun of righteousness will rise with healing in its wings, and the prophet Elijah will come before the great day of the Lord. It's the final word of the Old Testament, and it points straight at John the Baptist and Jesus.

WHY THIS MATTERS FOR YOU

You might be wondering why six short books written thousands of years ago to people in the ancient Near East have anything to say to your life. Here's why: the problems these prophets addressed haven't gone away.

People still wonder if God sees injustice. Habakkuk asked, and so do we. People still go through the motions of faith while their hearts are somewhere else. Malachi called it out, and we still need to hear it. People still feel overwhelmed by how small their efforts seem. Haggai and Zechariah spoke directly to that discouragement. And people still need to know that the story isn't over, that the silence isn't emptiness, that God is still working even when we can't see him.

These books also point relentlessly to Jesus. Habakkuk's declaration that the righteous will live by faith became the foundation of Paul's letter to the Romans. Zechariah's king on a donkey rode into Jerusalem on Palm Sunday. Zechariah's thirty pieces of silver landed in Judas' hands. Zechariah's struck shepherd was quoted by Jesus himself the night before he died. And Malachi's promise of Elijah was fulfilled in John the Baptist, the voice crying in the wilderness.

The Minor Prophets aren't minor. They're the final act before the curtain rises on the greatest story ever told.

BEFORE YOU START

These books contain intense material. There is graphic language about warfare and divine judgment. There are visions that can feel strange and disorienting. There are hard questions about why God allows suffering and how long justice takes to arrive.

The prophets don't soften their message for comfort, and neither will this book. But every difficult passage will be explained, and every hard truth will be connected to the larger story of a God who judges because he is just and saves because he loves.

Six prophets. Six messages. One story that stretches from the rubble of Nineveh to the edge of Bethlehem.

Let's hear what they have to say.

Turn the page.

1

THE GOD WHO DOESN'T FORGET

Have you ever dealt with a bully who seemed untouchable? Maybe it was a kid at school who said cruel things to people every single day and never got caught. The teachers didn't see it. The principal didn't know. Or maybe they knew and just didn't do anything. Every morning you'd walk into school wondering what this person would do next, and every afternoon you'd walk out thinking, *Does anyone even care? Is anything ever going to change?*

Now imagine that feeling lasting your entire life. Not just a school year. Your whole life. And not just your life, but your parents' lives, and your grandparents' lives, and their parents' lives before them. Imagine that the bully isn't a kid at school but an empire, the most powerful and most violent nation the ancient world had ever seen. Imagine that for over a hundred years, this empire has been terrorizing everyone around it, and no one can stop it.

That's what life was like for the people of Judah under the Assyrian Empire. And the book of Nahum is the moment when God finally said, "Enough."

THE EMPIRE EVERYONE FEARED

To understand Nahum, you need to understand Assyria. And to understand Assyria, you need to understand that they weren't just powerful. They were cruel in ways that are hard to even describe.

Assyria rose to dominance in the eighth century BC, and for the next hundred-plus years, they conquered everything in their path. Their capital city was Nineveh, one of the largest cities in the ancient world. Its walls stretched nearly eight miles around, enclosing palaces decorated with carved stone panels that depicted the king's military victories in vivid, horrifying detail.

And "horrifying" is the right word. Assyrian kings didn't just defeat their enemies. They wanted everyone to know what happened to people who resisted them. Their own royal inscriptions—the official records they were proud of—describe acts of brutality that would make your stomach turn. One king boasted about piling up the heads of his enemies at the gates of conquered cities. Another bragged about impaling hundreds of soldiers on stakes. They burned cities. They deported entire populations, ripping families from their homes and marching them hundreds of miles to foreign lands. They carved images of these horrors into the walls of their palaces so that every visiting diplomat would see them and think twice about rebellion.

This was the nation that had destroyed the northern kingdom of Israel in 722 BC. The ten northern tribes were conquered, scattered, and never returned. The southern kingdom of Judah survived, but only as a servant state, paying heavy tribute and living under constant threat. For generation after generation, the people of Judah went to sleep wondering if Assyria would come for them next.

And through all of it, God seemed silent.

A PROPHET NAMED "COMFORT"

Into this world of fear and oppression stepped a prophet named Nahum. We know almost nothing about him. He came from a town called Elkosh, but nobody knows exactly where that was. He probably lived in Judah, and he probably delivered his message sometime between 663 and 612 BC, during the final decades of Assyria's power.

Here's the irony: Nahum's name means "comfort." And his book, which is one of the darkest and most intense in the entire Bible, is exactly that. Not comfort for Nineveh. Comfort for everyone Nineveh had terrorized.

Nahum had one message, and he delivered it with the force of a sledgehammer: Nineveh is going to fall. God has seen everything. And he is coming to settle the account.

REMEMBER JONAH?

If the name Nineveh sounds familiar, it should. About a hundred years before Nahum, God sent another prophet to that same city. His name was Jonah, and you probably know his story. God told Jonah to go to Nineveh and warn them that judgment was coming. Jonah ran the other direction, got swallowed by a great fish, and eventually made it to Nineveh, where he delivered the shortest sermon in the Bible: "Forty more days and Nineveh will be overthrown."

And then something incredible happened. The people of Nineveh repented. From the king all the way down to the lowest citizen, they turned from their evil ways. God saw their repentance and relented. He did not destroy them. Jonah's story ended with mercy.

But mercy doesn't mean the story is over.

The repentance of Nineveh didn't last. Within a generation or two, Assyria was back to its old ways, more violent and more oppressive than ever. The empire that had been given a second chance used that chance to become even crueler. They conquered nation after nation, including the northern kingdom of Israel. They showed no mercy to the people of God.

Jonah was God's mercy. Nahum was God's justice. Same city. Same God. Two very different outcomes. And here's the lesson buried in the connection: God is patient. He is slow to anger. He gives people time to change. But patience has a purpose, and when that purpose has been exhausted, when every chance has been given and rejected, judgment comes.

Both Jonah and Nahum end with a question. Jonah ends with God asking, "Should I not have compassion on Nineveh?" Nahum ends with a question too: "Who has not felt your endless cruelty?" The first question invites mercy. The second explains why mercy has run out.

THE GOD WHO JUDGES

Nahum's book is only three chapters long, but every line hits hard. It opens not with Nineveh but with God. Before Nahum says a single word about armies or battles, he paints a picture of who God is, and it is terrifying.

"The LORD is a jealous and avenging God; the LORD takes vengeance and is filled with wrath."

That might not sound like the God you learned about in Sunday school. But keep reading. The very next verse says, "The LORD is slow to anger and great in power; the LORD will not leave the guilty unpunished."

Did you catch that? Slow to anger. Nahum isn't describing a God who flies off the handle. He is describing a God who has been patient for a very long time, who has given chance after chance, and who has finally reached the moment when justice can no longer wait.

Then Nahum describes God's power in images that would have shaken his audience. God rebukes the sea and dries it up. The mountains quake before him. The earth trembles at his presence. "Who can withstand his indignation? Who can endure his fierce anger?" The answer is obvious: nobody.

But right in the middle of this terrifying portrait, Nahum drops a single verse that changes everything: "The LORD is good, a refuge in times of trouble. He cares for those who trust in him."

That verse is the heart of the whole book. Yes, God is coming in judgment. Yes, his anger is real. But his anger is not aimed at everyone. It is aimed at the oppressor. For the people who have been living in fear, for the people who have been crushed under Assyria's boot, God's coming is not a threat. It is rescue.

The same storm that destroys the wicked shelters the righteous. That is who God is.

THE FALL OF THE UNTOUCHABLE CITY

The second and third chapters of Nahum describe the fall of Nineveh in some of the most vivid poetry in the Old Testament. Nahum writes as if he is watching it happen in real time, even though the city hadn't fallen yet when he spoke these words.

He describes attackers charging into the city: the crack of whips, the clatter of wheels, galloping horses, flashing swords. He describes the flooding of the river gates that protected the city, a detail that proved eerily accurate when Nineveh actually fell. He describes the looting of Nineveh's legendary wealth, gold and silver piled up over centuries of conquest. "Plunder the silver! Plunder the gold! The supply is endless."

Then Nahum does something bold. He reminds Nineveh of another city that thought it was untouchable: Thebes. Thebes was the great Egyptian city dedicated to the god Amun, protected by the Nile River and supported by powerful allies. And Assyria itself had conquered Thebes in 663 BC, carrying off its treasures and sending its people into exile. Nahum's point is devastating: if Thebes couldn't survive, what makes you think you can?

The final verses of the book are addressed directly to the king of Assyria. Your shepherds are asleep. Your people are scattered. Your wound is fatal.

And then the last line: "Everyone who hears the news about you claps their hands at your fall, for who has not felt your endless cruelty?"

That question hangs in the air. The answer, of course, is no one. Every nation in the ancient world had suffered at Assyria's hands. And when Nineveh finally fell, the whole world breathed a sigh of relief.

AND IT HAPPENED

In 612 BC, just as Nahum had prophesied, Nineveh fell. A combined army of Babylonians and Medes laid siege to the city. After about three months, the walls were breached. The city was looted, burned, and reduced to rubble. The Babylonian Chronicle, an ancient record preserved in the British Museum, describes the city being turned into "a hill of ruins and heaps of debris."

The destruction was so complete that within two hundred years, a Greek soldier named Xenophon marched past the site and didn't even know what it had been. The greatest city in the ancient world had been erased.

Nahum's prophecy came true, down to the details. The river gates were opened. The city was plundered. The defenders scattered. The king perished. Everything Nahum said would happen, happened. God's word proved reliable, even when it seemed impossible. At the height of Assyria's power, no one would have believed that Nineveh could fall. But Nahum believed it, because he knew the God who had spoken it.

WHAT THIS MEANS FOR US

First, God sees what the powerful do to the powerless. Assyria thought no one could hold them accountable. They were wrong. God was watching every act of cruelty, every innocent life destroyed, every nation trampled. He may not act on our timeline, but he never forgets and he never looks away. If you've ever been hurt by someone who seemed to get away with it, Nahum says: God sees. And he will act.

Second, patience is not the same as permission. God gave Nineveh over a hundred years between Jonah's visit and Nahum's prophecy. That was not God being okay with what they were doing. That was God being patient, giving them time to change. But patience that is wasted eventually gives way to justice. The fact that consequences haven't arrived yet doesn't mean they won't.

Third, the same God who judges is also a refuge. Nahum 1:7 is one of the most beautiful verses in the Old Testament, and it sits right in the middle of some of the most intense language about God's wrath. That's not an accident. It tells us that God's justice and God's goodness are not in conflict. They are two sides of the same character. The God who is furious at the oppressor is the same God who gently shelters the oppressed.

Fourth, no empire lasts forever. Assyria looked permanent. It had dominated the ancient world for over a century. Its cities were massive, its armies unbeatable, its wealth unimaginable. And it was erased so completely that people forgot where it had been. Every system built on cruelty and injustice has an expiration date. God is the only king whose rule never ends.

TALKING POINTS

1. **Nahum's name means "comfort," but his book is full of judgment.** How can a message about God's anger also be a message of comfort? Who would have found Nahum's words comforting, and why?

2. **God gave Nineveh a second chance through Jonah, but by Nahum's time that chance had been wasted.** What does this teach us about how God handles second chances? Is there a limit to God's patience?

3. **Nahum 1:7 says, "The LORD is good, a refuge in times of trouble. He cares for those who trust in him."** Why do you think this verse appears right in the middle of a passage about God's wrath? What does it tell us about how God treats different people differently?

4. **Assyria seemed invincible for over a century, but Nineveh was destroyed so completely that people forgot it existed.** Can you think of other examples from history where something that seemed permanent turned out to be temporary? What should that teach us about where we place our trust?

5. **Nahum ends with the question, "Who has not felt your endless cruelty?" The whole world celebrated Assyria's fall.** What does it tell us about the consequences of cruelty that even the most powerful nation in the world couldn't escape judgment for how it treated others?

The bully has been dealt with. But the questions Nahum raised—questions about justice and patience and what happens when the powerful abuse the powerless—are about to get even more personal. The next prophet won't be looking at a foreign enemy. He'll be looking straight up at God and asking the hardest question of all: Why do you let evil happen in the first place?

Turn the page.

2

THE PROPHET WHO ARGUED WITH GOD

When Thomas wakes up at the beginning of *The Maze Runner*, he has no memory of who he is or how he got there. He's surrounded by a group of boys trapped inside a massive, ever-shifting maze. Nobody knows why they're there. Nobody knows who put them there. And every night, the walls close and the maze fills with deadly creatures.

Thomas does what anyone would do. He starts asking questions. But every answer he gets makes things worse. The maze isn't just a prison. It's a test. The people who built it aren't trying to help. And the way out, when they finally find it, leads to something even more dangerous than what they were running from.

That's what it feels like to read the book of Habakkuk. A prophet looks at the world around him, sees terrible injustice, and does something most prophets never do: he argues with God. He asks the hard questions. And God answers. But God's answer doesn't make things better. It makes them worse. So the prophet argues again. And what follows is one of the most honest, raw, and ultimately beautiful conversations in the entire Bible.

A DIFFERENT KIND OF PROPHET

Most prophets in the Old Testament deliver God's message to the people. They stand in front of crowds and say, "This is what the Lord says." The people are the audience, and God is the one speaking through the prophet.

Habakkuk flips that around. Instead of speaking to the people on God's behalf, Habakkuk speaks to God on the people's behalf. He brings his complaints, his confusion, and his anger straight to the Almighty. And God, instead of shutting him down, actually engages in the conversation.

We know almost nothing about Habakkuk as a person. He's called "the prophet," which probably means he served in an official role, possibly connected to the temple in Jerusalem. He likely lived and ministered around 612–605 BC, which means he was a contemporary of Jeremiah. He lived in the final years of Judah's independence, after Assyria's power had crumbled but before Babylon had fully taken control of the region.

What we do know about Habakkuk comes from his words. And his words reveal a man who loved God deeply, cared about justice passionately, and wasn't afraid to say what he was really thinking, even when he was talking to the Creator of the universe.

THE FIRST QUESTION: WHY DON'T YOU DO SOMETHING?

The book opens with a cry that sounds like it's been building for a long time: "How long, LORD, must I call for help, but you do not listen?"

Habakkuk looks around at his own country, the kingdom of Judah, and sees a mess. The courts are corrupt. The powerful are exploiting the weak. Violence and injustice are everywhere.

The law has gone numb, and justice never seems to win. It's not that Habakkuk has just noticed the problem. The "How long?" tells us he's been praying about this for a while, begging God to intervene, and hearing nothing but silence.

If you've ever prayed for something important and felt like God wasn't listening, you know something of what Habakkuk felt. Maybe you prayed for a sick family member to get better. Maybe you asked God to fix a situation at home or at school. And nothing changed. The silence felt deafening.

Habakkuk takes that frustration and lays it right at God's feet. He doesn't pretend everything is fine. He doesn't slap on a fake smile and say, "I'm sure God has a plan." He says, "Why do you make me look at injustice? Why do you tolerate wrongdoing?" These are bold words to say to the God of the universe. But Habakkuk says them anyway.

GOD'S FIRST ANSWER: YOU WON'T BELIEVE THIS

God responds. But his response is not what Habakkuk expected. "Look at the nations and watch, and be utterly amazed. For I am going to do something in your days that you would not believe, even if you were told."

So far, so good. God is going to act. He's going to address the injustice. Habakkuk must have felt a surge of hope.

Then God explains his plan: "I am raising up the Babylonians, that ruthless and impetuous people, who sweep across the whole earth to seize dwellings not their own."

Imagine hearing that. Habakkuk asked God to deal with the corruption in Judah, and God said, "I will. I'm sending the most brutal army on earth to invade your country."

God then describes the Babylonians in terrifying detail. They are fiercer than wolves at dusk. Their cavalry gallops in from far away like eagles swooping down to devour. They gather prisoners like sand. They laugh at kings and mock fortified cities. They sweep past like the wind, guilty people whose own strength is their god.

This wasn't a rescue. It was a judgment. God wasn't going to fix the problem the way Habakkuk wanted. He was going to fix it by sending something far worse than what Habakkuk had complained about in the first place.

THE SECOND QUESTION: HOW CAN YOU DO THAT?

Now Habakkuk has a bigger problem. He asked why God tolerated injustice, and God told him he was sending the Babylonians to punish it. But the Babylonians were worse than the people they were coming to punish. How could a holy God use a wicked nation to destroy a less wicked nation? How could the cure be more deadly than the disease?

"Your eyes are too pure to look on evil," Habakkuk says to God. "You cannot tolerate wrongdoing. Why then do you tolerate the treacherous? Why are you silent while the wicked swallow up those more righteous than themselves?"

This is one of the deepest questions in the Bible. It's the question people ask after every war, every tragedy, every act of senseless cruelty: How can a good God allow this?

Habakkuk doesn't just throw up his hands and walk away. He does something remarkable. He says, "I will stand at my watch and station myself on the ramparts; I will look to see what he will say to me, and what answer I am to give to this complaint."

Picture that. The prophet climbs up to a watchtower and waits. He's not giving up. He's not pretending the question doesn't matter. He's planting himself in position and refusing to move until God answers.

GOD'S SECOND ANSWER: LIVE BY FAITH

God's response this time is different. Instead of a terrifying announcement, he gives Habakkuk a vision. And he tells him to write it down, to make it so clear that a messenger can run with it, because this vision isn't just for Habakkuk. It's for generations to come.

"The revelation awaits an appointed time; it speaks of the end and will not prove false. Though it linger, wait for it; it will certainly come and will not delay." Then comes the line that would echo through the rest of the Bible and change the world: "The righteous will live by his faithfulness."

That single sentence became one of the most quoted verses in all of Scripture. The apostle Paul built his entire letter to the Romans around it. He quoted it again in Galatians. The writer of Hebrews quoted it too. Martin Luther read it and it sparked the Protestant Reformation. One sentence from an obscure prophet in a tiny country changed the course of history.

But what does it mean? It means this: when everything around you is falling apart—when the answers don't make sense, when God's plan looks nothing like what you expected—the way forward is trust. Not blind trust that ignores reality. Habakkuk had been painfully honest about reality. It's a trust that says, "I don't understand what God is doing, but I know who God is, and that's enough."

The proud person trusts in himself. The faithful person trusts in God. And that trust, Habakkuk learned, is the only thing that will carry you through the darkness.

FIVE WOES AGAINST THE WICKED

God doesn't stop there. He goes on to pronounce five "woes" against the kind of evil that Babylon represents. These are sharp, almost mocking condemnations aimed at anyone who builds power through injustice.

Woe to the one who piles up stolen goods. Woe to the one who builds his house by unjust gain, trying to set his "nest on high" where no one can reach him. Woe to the one who builds a city with bloodshed. Woe to the one who degrades his neighbor. And woe to the one who trusts in lifeless idols instead of the living God.

Each woe carries the same message: what you have done to others will be done to you. The thief will be robbed. The exploiter will be exploited. The violent will face violence. God's justice may be slow, but it is certain.

The section ends with a verse that silences everything: "The LORD is in his holy temple; let all the earth be silent before him." After all the back-and-forth, all the arguing and questioning, God is still on his throne. He has not lost control. He has not forgotten. And every person and every nation will answer to him.

FROM TERROR TO TRUST

Chapter 3 is where Habakkuk's journey reaches its climax. He writes a prayer in the form of a psalm, designed to be sung in the temple with musical instruments. It's not a private journal entry. It's a song for the whole community to sing together in the dark years ahead.

The prayer opens with raw honesty: "LORD, I have heard of your fame; I stand in awe of your deeds, LORD. Repeat them in our day, in our time make them known; in wrath remember mercy."

Then Habakkuk describes a vision of God coming in power. Mountains tremble. Rivers split apart. The sun and moon stand still. God marches through the earth in fury, trampling nations, riding on horses and chariots of salvation. The imagery is massive, cosmic, overwhelming.

And Habakkuk's physical reaction is just as intense: "I heard and my heart pounded, my lips quivered at the sound; decay crept into my bones, and my legs trembled."

He is terrified. He knows what's coming for his people. He knows the Babylonians are on their way, and he knows God has ordained it. There will be war. There will be loss. There will be suffering.

And then come the most famous verses in the book. Maybe the most remarkable declaration of faith in the entire Old Testament: "Though the fig tree does not bud and there are no grapes on the vines, though the olive crop fails and the fields produce no food, though there are no sheep in the pen and no cattle in the stalls, yet I will rejoice in the LORD, I will be joyful in God my Savior. The Sovereign LORD is my strength; he makes my feet like the feet of a deer, he enables me to tread on the heights."

Read that again. Everything Habakkuk depended on for survival would be taken away. No figs, no grapes, no olives, no grain, no livestock. Total devastation. And in the face of all of it, he chooses joy. Not because things are good, but because God is good.

That's what faith looks like when it has been tested all the way to the bottom and still holds.

WHAT THIS MEANS FOR US

First, it's okay to bring your hardest questions to God. Habakkuk didn't get in trouble for asking "How long?" or "Why?" God didn't rebuke him for being honest. He answered him. If you're confused, angry, or frustrated with how things are going, you don't have to pretend everything is fine. God can handle your questions. He would rather have your honesty than your performance.

Second, God's answers don't always look the way we expect. Habakkuk wanted God to clean up Judah. God sent Babylon. Sometimes God works through circumstances that look like the opposite of what we prayed for. That doesn't mean he isn't working. It means his plan is bigger than ours.

Third, faith isn't a feeling. It's a decision. Habakkuk didn't feel confident at the end of his book. His heart was pounding. His legs were trembling. His bones felt like they were rotting. But he chose to trust God anyway. Faith isn't the absence of fear. It's trusting God in the middle of it.

Fourth, the righteous will live by faith. That one sentence from Habakkuk 2:4 became the foundation for the New Testament's teaching on salvation. Paul used it to explain that we are made right with God not by being perfect but by trusting him. It was true in Habakkuk's day, and it's true in ours. When you can't control the outcome, trust the one who can.

TALKING POINTS

1. **Habakkuk opened his book by asking God, "How long?"** Have you ever felt that way about something in your life? What did you do with that frustration? Did you bring it to God, or did you try to handle it on your own?

2. **God's answer to Habakkuk's first question made things harder, not easier.** Has God ever answered one of your prayers in a way you didn't expect? How did you respond?

3. **Habakkuk 2:4 says "the righteous will live by faith."** What do you think it means to "live by faith" on an ordinary Tuesday when nothing dramatic is happening? How is that different from living by faith during a crisis?

4. **The five woes describe people who build their lives on stolen goods, selfish ambition, violence, and idols.** What are some things people your age are tempted to build their identity on that won't last? What would it look like to build on something more solid?

5. **Habakkuk's final prayer says, "Though the fig tree does not bud ... yet I will rejoice in the LORD."** What would your version of that statement be? "Even if _________ happens, I will still trust God." What makes that kind of faith possible?

Habakkuk argued with God and didn't get easy answers. But he got something better: a faith strong enough to survive the worst that life could throw at him. The next prophet in line won't be arguing with God. He'll be delivering one of the most sweeping and urgent warnings in the entire Old Testament, a warning that reaches from the streets of Jerusalem to the farthest corners of the earth.

Turn the page.

3

THE DAY EVERYTHING RESETS

Early in *Jurassic Park*, the mathematician Ian Malcolm tries to warn everyone that the dinosaur theme park is a disaster waiting to happen. The scientists and engineers don't listen. They've built electric fences. They've installed tracking systems. They've thought of everything. John Hammond, the park's creator, keeps insisting that everything is under control.

Malcolm shakes his head. "The kind of control you're attempting is not possible," he says. The people in charge have convinced themselves they can manage forces far bigger than they are, and they've stopped asking whether they should.

Then the fences fail. The power goes out. And suddenly, creatures that were supposed to be safely contained are everywhere, and there is nowhere to hide. The whole park collapses not because of one big mistake but because of a deep, quiet arrogance that had been building the whole time: the assumption that nothing could go wrong.

The book of Zephaniah reads like God's version of that warning. An entire nation had convinced itself that everything was fine. Their leaders were corrupt. Their worship was polluted. And they had settled into a dangerous belief that God would never actually do anything about it. They thought the fences would hold.

They were wrong. And the prophet who came to tell them so delivered one of the most intense, sweeping, and ultimately hopeful messages in the entire Bible.

A PROPHET WITH CONNECTIONS

Zephaniah is one of the few prophets in the Bible whose family tree goes back four generations. Most prophets are identified by their father's name and nothing more. But Zephaniah's introduction traces his ancestry all the way back to a man named Hezekiah, who was almost certainly King Hezekiah, one of the greatest kings in Judah's history.

If that's right, then Zephaniah was royalty. He was a distant cousin of King Josiah, who was ruling Judah at the time. His royal connections would explain how he knew so much about the corruption inside the palace and the temple. He wasn't an outsider shouting from the street. He was an insider who could see firsthand how badly things had gone wrong.

His name means "the Lord hides," and some scholars think his parents gave him that name as a prayer. Zephaniah was probably born during the reign of Manasseh, one of Judah's worst kings, a man who promoted idol worship, persecuted the faithful, and even sacrificed children to foreign gods. Naming your son "the Lord hides" might have been a desperate plea: *Lord, hide this child. Protect him. Keep him safe in this terrible time.*

God did more than hide him. He gave him a message that would shake the nation.

Zephaniah likely preached sometime around 630–620 BC, during King Josiah's early reign but before Josiah's great religious reforms had fully taken hold. The country was still saturated with the idolatry and corruption that Manasseh had encouraged for over half a century. The temple was full of pagan objects. People were worshiping the stars on their rooftops. And the powerful were crushing the powerless without a second thought.

Into this mess, Zephaniah delivered a warning so intense that it would later inspire one of the most famous hymns in Christian history: the *Dies Irae*, the "Day of Wrath."

UN-CREATING THE WORLD

Zephaniah's opening words are staggering. Most prophets begin by targeting one nation, one sin, one problem. Zephaniah begins by targeting *everything*. "I will sweep away everything from the face of the earth," declares the Lord. "I will sweep away both man and beast; I will sweep away the birds in the sky and the fish in the sea."

Read that list carefully: humans, animals, birds, fish. That's the creation list from Genesis 1, but in reverse. God made fish, then birds, then animals, then humans. Now Zephaniah describes God removing humans, then animals, then birds, then fish. It's as if creation itself is being undone, rewound, taken apart piece by piece.

This isn't just judgment. It's un-creation. Zephaniah is saying that sin has so thoroughly corrupted the world that God is prepared to start over. If that sounds familiar, it should. The last time God responded this way was the flood in Genesis.

But then the focus narrows. After the cosmic sweep, Zephaniah zeroes in on Judah and Jerusalem. The problem isn't just "out there" in the world. It's right here, in God's own city, among God's own people.

THE SINS NOBODY TALKED ABOUT

Zephaniah calls out sin after sin, naming them with blunt precision. There were people who worshiped both the Lord and Baal, trying to have it both ways. There were people bowing down on their rooftops to worship the stars. There were people swearing oaths to the Lord and to Molech in the same breath, as if you could serve two gods at once.

Then Zephaniah targets a group that might surprise you: the complacent. These weren't the openly rebellious. They weren't bowing to idols or hurting anyone. They were just sitting there, doing nothing, convinced that God didn't care either way.

Zephaniah describes them this way: people who are "like wine left on its dregs, who think, 'The LORD will do nothing, either good or bad.'"

That image of wine left on its dregs is vivid. In the ancient world, if you left wine sitting too long without straining it, it would thicken and go stale. It wouldn't spoil dramatically. It would just slowly become worthless. That's what these people were like. Not actively wicked, just settled, comfortable, and completely indifferent to God. They assumed God was irrelevant, that he wouldn't act, that life would just keep rolling along the way it always had.

Zephaniah says those people are in just as much danger as

the idol worshipers. Because indifference to God isn't neutral. It's a slow-motion rebellion.

THE DAY OF THE LORD

Then comes the passage that made Zephaniah famous. Starting in 1:14, the prophet unleashes a description of the "day of the Lord" that is so intense, so relentless, that the words seem to stack on top of each other like waves crashing one after another.

"The great day of the LORD is near, near and coming quickly. The cry on the day of the LORD is bitter; the Mighty Warrior shouts his battle cry. That day will be a day of wrath, a day of distress and anguish, a day of trouble and ruin, a day of darkness and gloom, a day of clouds and blackness, a day of trumpet and battle cry."

Count the descriptions: wrath, distress, anguish, trouble, ruin, darkness, gloom, clouds, blackness, trumpet, battle cry. Zephaniah piles them up because no single word is enough. This day will be so overwhelming that language itself struggles to contain it.

And nothing will buy your way out. "Neither their silver nor their gold will be able to save them on the day of the LORD's wrath." Money, status, power, connections: none of it will matter. The playing field will be leveled completely.

JUDGMENT IN EVERY DIRECTION

Chapter 2 extends the warning beyond Judah to the surrounding nations. Zephaniah moves in all four compass directions: the Philistines to the west, Moab and Ammon to the east, Cush (Ethiopia) to the south, and Assyria to the north. No matter which way you look, judgment is coming.

The section on Assyria and Nineveh is especially pointed: "He will stretch out his hand against the north and destroy Assyria, leaving Nineveh utterly desolate and dry as the desert." As we saw in Nahum's prophecy, Nineveh seemed untouchable. Zephaniah agrees with Nahum: it won't last.

But before any of these judgment oracles, Zephaniah pauses to offer the most important invitation in the entire book: "Seek the LORD, all you humble of the land, you who do what he commands. Seek righteousness, seek humility; perhaps you will be sheltered on the day of the LORD's anger."

Notice that word: *perhaps*. Zephaniah doesn't guarantee escape. He doesn't promise that faithfulness will make everything easy. He says *perhaps*. That might sound discouraging, but it's actually deeply honest. It means that seeking God isn't a transaction where you put in good behavior and get protection in return. It's a relationship. You seek God because he is worth seeking, not because you're guaranteed a comfortable outcome. And those who seek him humbly, with no demands and no conditions, are exactly the kind of people God delights to shelter.

THE CITY THAT SHOULD HAVE KNOWN BETTER

Chapter 3 turns the spotlight back on Jerusalem, and the words are devastating. "Woe to the city of oppressors, rebellious and defiled! She obeys no one, she accepts no correction. She does not trust in the LORD, she does not draw near to her God."

Then comes the indictment of the leaders. Officials are roaring lions. Judges are evening wolves who leave nothing for morning. Prophets are reckless and treacherous. Priests violate the law they're supposed to guard.

And right in the middle of all this corruption, Zephaniah inserts one stunning verse: "The LORD within her is righteous; he does no wrong. Morning by morning he dispenses his justice, and every new day he does not fail."

God hasn't left. He's still there, in the middle of the mess, being faithful even when no one around him is. The corruption of Jerusalem's leaders doesn't change the character of the God who lives among them. He remains righteous. He remains consistent. Every single morning, he shows up. Every single day, he does not fail.

THE GOD WHO SINGS

After all the darkness, after pages of judgment and woe and fire, Zephaniah ends his book with one of the most astonishing passages in the entire Old Testament. "Sing, Daughter Zion; shout aloud, Israel! Be glad and rejoice with all your heart, Daughter Jerusalem! The LORD has taken away your punishment, he has turned back your enemy. The LORD, the King of Israel, is with you; never again will you fear any harm."

And then this: "The LORD your God is with you, the Mighty Warrior who saves. He will take great delight in you; in his love he will no longer rebuke you, but will rejoice over you with singing."

Stop and think about that. The God who just described himself shaking the foundations of the earth, pouring out wrath on nations, sweeping away everything from the face of the earth, that same God now *sings* over his people. Not a battle cry. Not a shout of fury. A song. A song of delight. A song of love.

Throughout the Bible, people sing to God. The Psalms are full of it. But here, God sings to his people. He rejoices over them with gladness. He exults over them with loud singing. The warrior who fights for his people is also the father who sings over his children.

This is the heart of Zephaniah's message. Yes, judgment is real. Yes, sin has consequences. Yes, the day of the Lord is coming and it is terrible. But on the other side of the fire, there is a God who saves the lame, gathers the outcast, and turns shame into praise. There is a God who brings his people home.

The book that began with un-creation ends with re-creation. The God who sweeps away also restores. The God who judges also sings.

WHAT THIS MEANS FOR US

First, complacency is more dangerous than you think. Zephaniah's harshest words weren't reserved for the worst sinners. They were aimed at people who just didn't care, people who assumed God was irrelevant and lived accordingly. Indifference to God isn't a safe middle ground. It's a slow slide toward everything Zephaniah warned about.

Second, no position of privilege makes you immune to judgment. Jerusalem was the city of God, the place where his temple stood. Its people assumed they were safe because of their address. Zephaniah shattered that assumption. Being close to God in name means nothing if you're far from him in practice.

Third, God is faithful even when everyone around him isn't. That verse about God being righteous "in her midst," doing justice every morning, is remarkable. It means that God doesn't abandon corrupt institutions or broken communities. He stays. He keeps being who he is. And that faithfulness is what makes restoration possible.

Fourth, God's ultimate goal is not destruction but joy. Zephaniah's book moves from wrath to singing, from un-creation to restoration. That's the trajectory of the whole Bible: God is always working toward the day when he can rejoice over his people and they can rejoice in him. The judgment is real, but it's not the last word. The song is.

TALKING POINTS

1. **Zephaniah describes people who think "the LORD will do nothing, either good or bad."** Why is that attitude so dangerous? Do you see that kind of indifference toward God in the world today? In yourself?

2. **The leaders of Jerusalem were supposed to protect the people but instead became their worst oppressors.** What does this teach us about the responsibility that comes with leadership? How can leaders today guard against the same kind of corruption?

3. **Zephaniah 2:3 says to "seek the LORD" and "perhaps you will be sheltered."** Why do you think the prophet says "perhaps" instead of making a guarantee? What does that tell us about what it means to trust God?

4. **Zephaniah says God is righteous "in her midst," faithful every morning even while surrounded by corruption.** What does it mean to you that God stays present even in broken places? How does that change how you think about difficult situations in your own life?

5. Zephaniah 3:17 says God "will rejoice over you with singing." What do you think it means that God sings over his people? How does that picture of God compare to how you usually think about him?

The prophet of wrath has become the prophet of song. God's judgment is real, but so is his joy, and the joy gets the last word. The next voice we'll hear belongs to a prophet from a completely different era, one who speaks not to a people waiting for judgment but to a people who have already survived it and come home. The question now is: What do you do with a second chance?

Turn the page.

4

THE PROPHET WHO GOT PEOPLE MOVING

Have you ever had something important you knew you needed to do, but you kept putting it off? Maybe it was a school project that was due in two weeks. You had plenty of time. So instead of starting it, you organized your desk. You cleaned your room. You rearranged your bookshelf. You did a dozen other things that felt productive but weren't the thing. And then one morning you woke up and the project was due tomorrow and you hadn't started.

Here's the strange part. While you were avoiding that project, nothing else felt right either. You couldn't fully enjoy the stuff you were doing instead, because in the back of your mind you knew you were ignoring the thing that actually mattered. The avoidance was like a low hum in the background of your life, draining the satisfaction out of everything.

Now imagine an entire nation doing that for eighteen years.

That's the book of Haggai. And the message God sent through this prophet is as practical and direct as anything in the Bible: Stop making excuses. Stop putting yourself first. Get to work on what matters. And watch what happens when you do.

THE STORY SO FAR

To understand Haggai, you need to know what had happened to the people of Judah in the decades before he showed up.

In 586 BC, the Babylonians destroyed Jerusalem. They burned the temple Solomon had built, tore down the city walls, and dragged most of the population into exile. For nearly fifty years, the Jewish people lived in Babylon, far from home, longing for the day God would bring them back.

Then, in 539 BC, the Persian king Cyrus conquered Babylon and issued an extraordinary decree: the Jewish exiles could go home. They could return to Jerusalem and rebuild the temple of their God. Cyrus even provided financial support for the project.

Thousands of Jews made the long journey back. When they arrived, one of the first things they did was lay the foundation for a new temple. It was a deeply emotional moment. The younger people cheered because something was finally being built. The older people, the ones who remembered Solomon's temple, wept because they could see how much smaller this new beginning would be.

But then something went wrong. Opposition came from neighboring peoples who didn't want Jerusalem rebuilt. The work slowed. Then it stopped. And for eighteen years, the half-built temple sat there, abandoned, while the people turned their attention to their own lives.

By 520 BC, the people had settled in. They had built homes for themselves. Some had even paneled their houses with wood, a finishing touch that showed real comfort. Meanwhile, the temple of the living God sat in ruins in the middle of the city like a rotting tooth nobody wanted to deal with.

That's when Haggai stepped onto the scene.

"CONSIDER YOUR WAYS"

We know almost nothing about Haggai the man. His name means "festal," possibly suggesting he was born during one of Israel's great festivals. He's called "the prophet," and his messages are dated with remarkable precision. Everything recorded in his book happened within a four-month window in 520 BC, from late August to mid-December. It's the most precisely dated book in the entire Bible.

But what Haggai lacked in biographical detail, he made up for in directness. His first message cut straight to the heart of the problem. "This is what the LORD Almighty says: 'These people say, "The time has not yet come to rebuild the LORD's house."'"

The people had a reasonable excuse. The economy was bad. Times were hard. There was still so much personal rebuilding to do. Surely God understood that the temple could wait until things stabilized.

God's response through Haggai was blunt: "Is it a time for you yourselves to be living in your paneled houses, while this house remains a ruin?"

Then came the phrase Haggai repeated like a drumbeat throughout his ministry: "Give careful thought to your ways." Look at your life. Examine your priorities. Consider whether your current strategy is actually working.

And here's where Haggai got painfully specific: "You have planted much, but harvested little. You eat, but never have enough. You drink, but never have your fill. You put on clothes, but are not warm. You earn wages, only to put them in a purse with holes in it."

A purse with holes. That image is so vivid it has stuck with readers for over 2,500 years. You work hard. You earn money. But somehow it's never enough. Something keeps draining it away. No matter how much effort you put in, the results feel hollow.

Haggai's explanation was simple: this wasn't bad luck. It was cause and effect. The people had put their own comfort first and God's house last, and the result was a life that never quite felt satisfying. They were experiencing the ancient covenant curses Moses had warned about in Deuteronomy: poor harvests, drought, and frustration would follow those who abandoned their priorities with God.

The solution was equally simple: "Go up into the mountains and bring down timber and build the house, so that I may take pleasure in it and be honored."

SOMETHING REMARKABLE HAPPENED

Here's the part that makes Haggai different from almost every other prophet in the Old Testament: the people listened.

In most prophetic books, the prophet delivers God's message and the people ignore it, argue with it, or try to kill the messenger. The history of Israel is largely a history of prophets being rejected.

But not this time. "Then Zerubbabel son of Shealtiel, Joshua son of Jozadak, the high priest, and the whole remnant of the people obeyed the voice of the LORD their God and the message of the prophet Haggai."

The governor obeyed. The high priest obeyed. The people obeyed. Within twenty-three days of Haggai's first message, work on the temple had begun. After eighteen years of excuses and delays, the entire community got up and started building.

And God responded immediately with the shortest and sweetest promise in the book: "I am with you."

Four words. That was enough. The God whose house they had neglected for almost two decades didn't lecture them about how long it had taken. He didn't hold a grudge. The moment they turned back to him, he was there. "I am with you." That's grace.

"THE GLORY OF THIS HOUSE"

About a month after the work began, discouragement set in. Some of the older people who remembered Solomon's temple looked at what was being built and felt sick. The original temple had been one of the wonders of the ancient world, covered in gold and cedar, filled with the visible glory of God. This new structure looked like a shack by comparison.

God addressed their discouragement head-on through Haggai: "Who of you is left who saw this house in its former glory? How does it look to you now? Does it not seem to you like nothing?"

He acknowledged their disappointment. He didn't pretend the new temple was as grand as the old one. But then he said something that changed everything. "Be strong, all you people of the land, and work. For I am with you. This is what I covenanted with you when you came out of Egypt. And my Spirit remains among you. Do not fear."

The message was clear: what made the temple glorious was never the gold or the cedar. It was God's presence. And God was promising to be present in this smaller, humbler building just as he had been in Solomon's magnificent one.

Then Haggai looked even further ahead. God promised that "in a little while" he would shake the heavens and the earth, and the nations would bring their wealth, and the glory of this new house would surpass the glory of the former one. The writer of Hebrews in the New Testament would later pick up this promise and connect it to the coming of Jesus and his unshakable kingdom.

The point for Haggai's audience was this: don't despise small beginnings. What looks insignificant now is part of something much bigger than you can see. God's plans extend far beyond what you can build with your hands.

A LESSON ABOUT HOLINESS

Haggai's third message came on December 18, 520 BC, and it involved a pop quiz for the priests.

He asked them a question about the law: If someone carries consecrated meat in the fold of their garment, and that garment touches bread or stew or wine, does the food become holy? The priests answered correctly: no. Holiness doesn't transfer that easily. You can't make something sacred just by touching it to something sacred.

Then Haggai asked a second question: If someone who is ceremonially unclean from touching a dead body touches any of those same foods, do they become unclean? The priests answered again: yes. Defilement spreads much more easily than holiness does.

Then Haggai applied the lesson. The people were like the second scenario. Their neglect of God's house had left them in a state of spiritual contamination, and that contamination had spread to everything they did. Their offerings, their work, their daily lives, all of it was affected by their misplaced priorities.

But now that they had turned back and started building, God made a promise: "From this day on I will bless you." The curse was being reversed. The drought and disappointment that had marked the previous eighteen years were coming to an end. Obedience was opening the door to blessing.

THE SIGNET RING

Haggai's final message came on the same day as the third, and it was addressed directly to Zerubbabel, the governor. Zerubbabel was a descendant of King David, the grandson of King Jehoiachin, who had been carried off to Babylon. Years earlier, the prophet Jeremiah had pronounced a devastating judgment on Jehoiachin: "Even if you were a signet ring on my right hand, I would still pull you off."

A signet ring was a king's seal of authority. Jeremiah was saying that God was revoking the royal authority of David's line. The ring was coming off.

Now, through Haggai, God reversed that judgment. He told Zerubbabel: "I will take you, my servant, and I will make you like my signet ring, for I have chosen you."

The ring was going back on. The line of David, which had seemed broken and finished, was being restored. Zerubbabel would not become a political king in the way David had been. But the line he represented would continue, generation after generation, all the way to a carpenter's son born in Bethlehem who would be the true and final King.

Haggai's last recorded word is a word of hope: "I have chosen you." After exile, after ruin, after eighteen years of neglect, God was still choosing his people, still keeping his promises, still moving his plan forward.

WHAT THIS MEANS FOR US

First, misplaced priorities have real consequences. The people in Haggai's day weren't doing anything obviously evil. They were building homes, planting crops, earning wages. Good things. But they had made good things the main thing, and the result was a life that felt empty no matter how hard they worked. When God's priorities aren't our priorities, even our successes feel hollow.

Second, it's never too late to start. Eighteen years is a long time to procrastinate. But God didn't say, "You've waited too long. Forget it." He said, "Start now." The moment the people turned back and began to work, God met them with presence and blessing. If you've been avoiding something God has put on your heart, the best time to start was years ago. The second-best time is today.

Third, don't despise small beginnings. The new temple looked like nothing compared to Solomon's. But God's plans for that humble building were bigger than anyone could see. If what you're building for God looks small and unimpressive, take heart. God has never been limited by the size of what his people can offer.

Fourth, God's presence matters more than the package

it comes in. The gold and cedar of Solomon's temple were beautiful, but they weren't what made it holy. God's presence was. And God promised to be just as present in a small, simple building as he had been in the grandest structure on earth. The same is true for us. God isn't looking for impressive packaging. He's looking for willing hearts.

TALKING POINTS

1. **The people in Haggai's day had a reasonable excuse for not building the temple: times were hard and there was too much else to do.** What kinds of "reasonable excuses" do people use today for putting off what God wants them to do?

2. **Haggai describes earning "wages to put them in a purse with holes."** Have you ever experienced something like that, where you worked hard but the results felt empty? What do you think was missing?

3. **The people of Judah actually listened to Haggai and obeyed.** What do you think made the difference this time, compared to all the times Israel ignored the prophets?

4. **God told the discouraged builders, "The glory of this present house will be greater than the glory of the former house."** How do you think the people felt hearing that? Have you ever started something that looked small but turned into something bigger than you expected?

5. **God reversed the curse on Jehoiachin's line by calling Zerubbabel his "signet ring."** What does it tell you about God that he reverses judgments and restores broken lines? How does that connect to the story of Jesus?

Haggai got the people moving. The temple walls were rising. The foundation was laid. But the work was far from finished, and the questions facing this fragile community were far from answered. The next prophet would pick up where Haggai left off, with visions so strange and beautiful that they would point all the way from a half-built temple in Jerusalem to a king riding on a donkey and a shepherd struck down for his sheep.

Turn the page.

5

VISIONS IN THE NIGHT

Early in *Spirited Away*, a ten-year-old girl named Chihiro walks through a tunnel and finds herself in a world that makes no sense. A bathhouse the size of a palace serves spirits she can't identify. A giant baby fills an entire room. A creature with no face follows her around, offering gold that turns to mud. Paper birds chase people through the sky. A river god arrives caked in centuries of garbage, and the staff has to pull a bicycle out of him.

Nothing in this world works the way Chihiro expects. But here's what she discovers as the story unfolds: the strange world has its own logic. The bizarre creatures have reasons for being what they are. The rules are different from what she's used to, but they aren't random. And once she learns to see the world on its own terms instead of hers, everything starts to click into place.

The first six chapters of Zechariah are a bit like stepping into that bathhouse. In a single night, the prophet receives eight visions, and they are some of the strangest scenes in all of Scripture. Horses of different colors patrolling the earth. A high priest standing in filthy clothes while an angel changes his outfit. A golden lampstand fed by two olive trees. A giant flying scroll. A woman stuffed into a basket and carried off by figures with wings like storks. Four chariots pulled by horses charging out from between two bronze mountains.

If you read those visions without any explanation, they sound bizarre. But each one has a specific meaning, and when you put them together, they tell one of the most hopeful stories in the Bible: God is coming back to his people, and nothing can stop him.

THE PROPHET AND HIS MOMENT

Zechariah was a younger contemporary of Haggai. Both prophets lived in Jerusalem around 520 BC, and both were deeply involved in getting the temple rebuilt after the Babylonian exile. But where Haggai was blunt and practical ("Stop making excuses and build"), Zechariah was a visionary. His messages were filled with symbols, images, and pictures that stretched far beyond the immediate building project to the distant future.

Zechariah came from a priestly family. He was both a priest and a prophet, which made him uniquely positioned to speak about the temple, the sacrificial system, and the coming Messiah. His name means "the Lord remembers," which is fitting, because his entire book is about God remembering his promises and following through on them.

The book of Zechariah is the longest of the Minor Prophets and, after the Psalms, the most quoted part of the Old Testament in the Gospel accounts of Jesus' death and resurrection. If you want to understand the events of Holy Week, you need to know Zechariah.

But before we get to those later chapters, we need to start where Zechariah started: with a call to repentance and a night full of visions.

DON'T BE LIKE YOUR ANCESTORS

Zechariah's first recorded message, delivered in late October or early November of 520 BC, was a warning: "Do not be like your ancestors, to whom the earlier prophets proclaimed: 'Turn from your evil ways and your evil practices.' But they would not listen or pay attention to me, declares the LORD."

The point was sharp. The previous generations had ignored every prophet God sent. Isaiah, Jeremiah, Ezekiel: they all warned that disaster was coming if the people didn't change. The people didn't change. And the disaster came. Jerusalem fell. The temple burned. The nation went into exile.

Now a new generation was back in the land, trying to start over. Zechariah's opening message was simple: You have a chance your ancestors wasted. Don't make the same mistake. Return to God, and he will return to you.

EIGHT VISIONS IN ONE NIGHT

About three months later, in February of 519 BC, Zechariah received eight visions in a single night. An angel stood beside him, explaining each scene as it unfolded. Together, the visions tell a connected story: God is taking back his city, cleansing his people, empowering his leaders, removing wickedness, and sending his forces to establish justice across the earth.

Here are the visions that matter most for understanding Zechariah's message.

The Horsemen Among the Myrtle Trees (1:7–17). In the first vision, Zechariah sees a man riding a red horse, standing among myrtle trees in a ravine. Behind him are riders on red, brown, and white horses. They've been patrolling the earth on God's behalf, and they report back: "We have gone throughout the earth and found the whole world at rest and in peace."

That sounds like good news, but it isn't. The world is at rest because the Persian Empire has everything under control. Meanwhile, God's people are still struggling in a half-rebuilt city. The nations that crushed Israel are comfortable and prosperous. Where is the justice?

The angel of the Lord asks the question everyone was thinking: "LORD Almighty, how long will you withhold mercy from Jerusalem?"

God's answer is immediate and tender. He speaks "kind and comforting words." He declares that he is deeply concerned for Jerusalem, that he is angry with the comfortable nations who went too far in punishing his people, and that he is returning to Jerusalem with mercy. The temple will be rebuilt. The city will overflow with prosperity. God will comfort his people and choose Jerusalem again.

The very first vision, in other words, is an announcement: the exile is over. God is coming home.

The Filthy Garments of Joshua (3:1–10). The fourth vision is the most dramatic of all. Zechariah sees Joshua the high priest standing before the angel of the Lord. And standing beside him, ready to accuse, is Satan.

Joshua is wearing filthy clothes. The word in the original language is graphic: the clothes are covered in what amounts to human waste. This is the high priest, the man responsible for standing before God on behalf of the entire nation, and he's dressed in filth. He's unfit. Unclean. Disqualified.

Satan is there to make exactly that case. And honestly, he has a point. The people of Judah had spent generations in rebellion. Their exile was their own fault. They were spiritually contaminated, and their high priest's filthy garments were a picture of the whole nation's condition.

But God doesn't let Satan finish. "The LORD rebuke you, Satan! Is not this man a burning stick snatched from the fire?"

Then God does something breathtaking. He orders the filthy clothes removed. "See, I have taken away your sin," he says. And he has Joshua dressed in rich, clean garments, with a clean turban placed on his head. In a single act, God strips away the shame and replaces it with dignity. He doesn't wait for Joshua to clean himself up. He does it for him.

This vision is one of the clearest pictures of grace in the Old Testament. The accusation was valid. The guilt was real. But God chose mercy over condemnation. He took away the filth and clothed his priest in garments fit for service.

Then God makes a promise: he is going to bring his servant, "the Branch." That title, the Branch, is a code name for the coming Messiah, a future king from David's line who will combine the roles of king and priest. And on the day the Branch comes, God says, he will "remove the sin of this land in a single day."

One day. All the sin of the land, gone. Zechariah's audience couldn't have fully understood what that meant. But centuries later, on a Friday afternoon outside Jerusalem, it happened.

The Lampstand and the Olive Trees (4:1–14). In the fifth vision, Zechariah sees a golden lampstand, like the one in the temple, with a bowl on top and seven lamps. On either side of the lampstand stand two olive trees, feeding oil into the bowl through golden pipes. The lampstand never runs out of fuel because it's constantly being supplied from outside itself.

Zechariah asks what this means, and the angel delivers one of the most famous verses in the Bible: "Not by might nor by power, but by my Spirit, says the LORD Almighty."

The message was aimed at Zerubbabel, who was leading the temple construction. The obstacles were enormous. The community was small and poor. The work seemed impossible. But God was saying: this project will not succeed because of human strength or political connections. It will succeed because my Spirit is powering it. Like the lampstand that never runs dry, the work of God is sustained by a supply that comes from God himself.

Then comes another verse that has comforted discouraged people for centuries: "Who dares despise the day of small things?"

Everything about their situation looked small. A small community. A small city. A small temple. But God was not measuring by human standards. What looked like a day of small things was the beginning of something that would eventually fill the earth.

The Flying Scroll and the Woman in the Basket (5:1–11). The sixth and seventh visions deal with something the returned exiles needed to hear: wickedness will not be tolerated in the new community. A massive flying scroll represents God's law going out to judge thieves and liars. Then, in an even stranger image, a woman representing wickedness is stuffed into a measuring basket, sealed with a lead cover, and carried away by two winged figures to the land of Babylon.

The message is vivid and almost funny in its directness. God is cleaning house. Wickedness, the very thing that got the people exiled in the first place, is being physically removed from the land and dumped back in Babylon where it belongs. God isn't just bringing his people back. He's making sure the poison that destroyed them before doesn't come back with them.

The Four Chariots (6:1–8). The final vision mirrors the first. In the opening vision, horses patrolled the earth and reported that everything was quiet. Now, in the closing vision, four chariots burst out from between two bronze mountains, pulled by powerful horses, and charge across the earth in every direction. These are God's heavenly forces going out to subdue the nations and establish his justice.

The eight visions form a complete picture. God has returned. His people are cleansed. His temple is being built by his Spirit. Wickedness is removed. And his forces are going out to deal with every nation that opposes him. From start to finish, the visions declare one thing: God is in control, and his kingdom is coming.

THE CROWN AND THE BRANCH

Immediately after the eight visions, God tells Zechariah to do something unusual. He's to take silver and gold, make a crown, and place it on the head of Joshua the high priest. Not on Zerubbabel the governor, the descendant of David. On Joshua, the priest.

Then God says: "Here is the man whose name is the Branch, and he will branch out from his place and build the temple of the LORD. He will be clothed with majesty and will sit and rule on his throne. And he will be a priest on his throne."

A priest on a throne. A king who is also a priest. In Israel's history, those two roles had always been separate. Kings came from the tribe of Judah. Priests came from the tribe of Levi. Nobody was supposed to be both. But Zechariah is pointing to a future figure who will unite the two roles in one person: a king who rules with authority and a priest who makes people right with God.

That figure is the Branch. And the New Testament identifies him clearly: Jesus of Nazareth, the king who died as a sacrifice for his people and rose to reign forever.

WHAT THIS MEANS FOR US

First, God sees what you can't see. Zechariah's visions pulled back the curtain on a reality that was invisible to the struggling community in Jerusalem. While they saw poverty and rubble, God saw horsemen patrolling the earth, chariots enforcing justice, and a plan unfolding exactly on schedule. When your life feels chaotic and directionless, there is more going on than you can see.

Second, God removes your shame before you can fix it yourself. Joshua didn't clean his own clothes. He couldn't. He stood there in filth, and God stripped it off and dressed him in something clean. That's the gospel in a single scene. You don't have to get yourself together before coming to God. He does the cleaning. You just have to stand there and let him.

Third, what matters is God's Spirit, not your strength.

"Not by might nor by power, but by my Spirit." The work God calls you to do will not succeed because you're talented enough, popular enough, or strong enough. It will succeed because God's Spirit supplies what you lack. Stop measuring your resources and start trusting his.

Fourth, don't despise small beginnings. If what you're doing for God looks small and unimpressive right now, you're in good company. So did the rebuilt temple. So did a handful of returned exiles in a ruined city. God has a long history of building enormous things from tiny starting points.

TALKING POINTS

1. **Zechariah's visions used strange images to communicate deep truths.** Why do you think God sometimes speaks in pictures and symbols instead of plain language? What are the advantages of learning through images?

2. **In the vision of Joshua's filthy garments, Satan accused the high priest and God silenced the accusation.** How does it feel to know that when you fail, God's response is to remove your shame rather than pile on more guilt? How does this connect to what Jesus did?

3. **"Not by might nor by power, but by my Spirit."** What situation in your life right now feels too big for your own strength? What would it look like to trust God's Spirit to work through you instead of relying only on yourself?

4. **God asked, "Who dares despise the day of small things?"** Is there something in your life or your faith that feels small and insignificant? How does Zechariah's message change the way you see it?

5. The Branch is described as both a king and a priest. Why is it important that Jesus fills both roles? What does it mean for you that the same person who rules with authority also stands before God on your behalf?

Zechariah's night visions showed a world behind the world, where God was actively fighting for his people, cleansing their sin, and building his kingdom one stone at a time. But the prophet's message wasn't finished. The visions gave way to harder questions about what God really wanted from his people, and to a prophecy about a king unlike any king anyone had ever imagined.

Turn the page.

6

THE KING NOBODY EXPECTED

Queen of Katwe tells the true story of Phiona Mutesi, a girl growing up in one of the poorest slums in Kampala, Uganda. Her family lives in a single-room shack. She sells maize on the street to survive. She has almost no formal education. Nobody looks at Phiona and sees a future champion of anything.

Then she discovers chess. A local missionary runs a sports program in the slum, and Phiona wanders in one day and starts learning the game. At first, she's just another kid from Katwe. But she has something nobody expected: a mind that sees the board differently. She starts winning. Then she keeps winning. She enters tournaments against kids from wealthy schools who have been trained for years, kids with coaches and equipment and every advantage in the world, and she beats them.

By the end of the film, Phiona is competing internationally and dreaming of becoming a grandmaster. The girl from the slum turned out to be the most formidable player in the room. Not because she had the most resources. Not because she looked the part. But because real strength had nothing to do with what the world expected it to look like.

That's the surprise at the heart of Zechariah 7–10. The people of Judah were looking for a powerful king who would crush their enemies and restore their nation to glory. What God described instead was a king who arrives riding on a donkey. And that king, the humble one, the one nobody expected, turned out to be the most powerful king the world has ever known.

A QUESTION ABOUT FASTING

Two years into the temple reconstruction, in December of 518 BC, a delegation arrived in Jerusalem from the town of Bethel with a question for the priests and prophets: "Should we keep fasting?"

For decades, the people of Judah had been observing special fasts to mourn the destruction of Jerusalem and the temple. They fasted in the fourth month to remember the day the Babylonian army breached the walls. They fasted in the fifth month to remember the burning of the temple. They fasted in the seventh month to remember the assassination of Gedaliah, the governor appointed after the fall. They fasted in the tenth month to remember the start of the siege.

Now that the temple was being rebuilt, the question seemed reasonable: Do we still need to mourn? Isn't the crisis over?

God's answer, delivered through Zechariah, cut deeper than anyone expected. He didn't say yes or no to the fasting. He changed the subject entirely.

"When you fasted and mourned, was it really for me that you fasted? And when you were eating and drinking, were you not just feasting for yourselves?"

In other words: your fasts were never really about me. You went through the motions of mourning, but your heart wasn't in it. And that's the same problem your ancestors had. They performed religious rituals while ignoring what God actually cared about.

WHAT GOD REALLY WANTS

Then Zechariah spelled out exactly what God did care about, using language that echoed the prophets who came before him: "Administer true justice; show mercy and compassion to one another. Do not oppress the widow or the fatherless, the foreigner or the poor. Do not plot evil against each other."

This wasn't new. Amos had said the same thing. Micah had said the same thing. Isaiah had said the same thing. For centuries, God had been telling his people that what he wanted wasn't better rituals. It was better character. Not more impressive worship services, but more genuine love for their neighbors.

The ancestors hadn't listened. "They refused to pay attention; stubbornly they turned their backs and covered their ears." So God scattered them among the nations, and the pleasant land became desolate.

Zechariah's point was sharp: Don't repeat the mistake. The question isn't whether to fast or not to fast. The question is whether you're becoming the kind of people God actually wants you to be. Religious activity without justice and compassion is just noise.

A CITY OF JOY

After the rebuke came one of the most beautiful visions in the Old Testament. In chapter 8, God delivered ten promises of blessing, each one beginning with "This is what the LORD Almighty says." Together, they paint a picture of what Jerusalem was meant to become.

"Old men and women will again sit in the streets of Jerusalem, each of them with cane in hand because of their age. The city streets will be filled with boys and girls playing there."

Think about what that picture means. In times of war and famine, the elderly and children are the most vulnerable. They're the first to suffer. But in the restored Jerusalem Zechariah describes, old people sit peacefully in the sun, and kids play in the streets without fear. It's a picture of total safety. Total peace. A city where the most fragile members of the community can thrive.

And this restoration wouldn't be limited to God's people. Zechariah saw a day when people from many nations and languages would come to Jerusalem, saying, "Let us go with you, because we have heard that God is with you." Ten people from different nations would grab hold of one Jewish person and say, "Take us with you. We want to know your God."

The fasts that had marked decades of mourning? God promised they would become "joyful and glad occasions and happy festivals." Weeping would turn to celebration. Mourning would become feasting. The story wasn't ending in grief. It was heading somewhere breathtaking.

THE KING ON A DONKEY

Then, in chapter 9, Zechariah delivered the prophecy that would echo through the centuries and land directly in the streets of Jerusalem on the first Palm Sunday.

The chapter begins with God sweeping through the nations surrounding Israel. From Damascus in the north to the Philistine cities along the coast, God moves through the land, stripping away the power of Israel's enemies and claiming the territory for himself. It reads like a military campaign, and anyone listening would have felt their pulse quicken. This was the moment. God was finally going to establish his kingdom and put a real king on the throne.

Then came the verse that nobody saw coming: "Rejoice greatly, Daughter Zion! Shout, Daughter Jerusalem! See, your king comes to you, righteous and victorious, lowly and riding on a donkey, on a colt, the foal of a donkey."

A donkey.

Not a warhorse. Not a chariot. A donkey. The animal associated with humble service, not military conquest. The kind of mount a farmer would ride to market, not a king would ride into battle.

But this wasn't weakness disguised as strength. This was a completely different kind of strength. This king would be "righteous," meaning he would set things right. He would be "victorious," but victorious through God's power, not through military force. He would be "lowly," or afflicted, someone who knew suffering from the inside.

And this king's mission? "He will proclaim peace to the nations, and his rule will extend from sea to sea and from the ends of the earth." Not a kingdom built by swords. A kingdom built by peace. Not dominion seized through violence. Dominion extended through the kind of humble, self-giving love that the world has never been able to overcome.

Five centuries later, Jesus of Nazareth rode a donkey into Jerusalem while crowds waved palm branches and shouted. All four Gospel writers record the moment, and Matthew and John both quote Zechariah 9:9 directly. What the crowd didn't fully understand yet was that this humble king would proclaim peace not by defeating Rome but by dying on a cross and rising from the dead. The kingdom he was building couldn't be stopped by armies, because it wasn't built with armies. It was built with grace.

THE SHEPHERD WHO GATHERS

Chapter 10 shifts the imagery from king to shepherd, but the message is the same. God looks at his people, scattered and oppressed, and is filled with compassion. "My anger burns against the shepherds," he says, referring to the leaders, both foreign rulers and corrupt domestic officials, who have failed the people.

God promises to care for his flock personally. He will raise up new leaders from among his own people. He will strengthen both the southern kingdom (Judah) and the remnants of the northern kingdom (the tribes of Joseph). He will gather them from the nations where they've been scattered, redeem them, and bring them home.

The language echoes the exodus. God's people will pass through the sea again, like they did when they left Egypt. The proud nations that held them captive will be humbled. And God's people, once weak and scattered, will be strong.

"I will strengthen them in the LORD and in his name they will live securely." It's the shepherd language that Jesus would later take for himself. "I am the good shepherd," he said. "The good shepherd lays down his life for the sheep." The king on the donkey and the shepherd who gathers the scattered flock are the same person. And he was already on his way.

WHAT THIS MEANS FOR US

First, God cares more about your character than your religious activity. Fasting, praying, going to church, reading your Bible: none of these are bad things. But if they're disconnected from how you treat people, they're empty. God wants justice, mercy, and compassion. Those aren't extras. They're the main thing.

Second, God's vision for the future includes everyone being safe. Old people sitting peacefully, children playing without fear. That vision should shape how we act now. Every act of kindness, every stand for justice, every time you look out for someone weaker than you—you're participating in the kind of world God is building.

Third, God's power often looks nothing like the world's power. The world expected a conquering king. God sent a man on a donkey. The world expects strength to look like force. God says strength looks like humility, service, and self-giving love. If you want to be powerful the way God defines power, start by being willing to look small.

Fourth, God doesn't forget his scattered people. If you feel lost, overlooked, or far from where you're supposed to be, Zechariah 10 is for you. God's eyes are on every person who belongs to him, no matter how far away they've drifted. He is the shepherd who goes looking. He is the God who brings people home.

TALKING POINTS

1. **God told the people their fasts were really about themselves, not about him.** How can you tell the difference between religious activity that's genuine and religious activity that's just going through the motions?

2. **Zechariah's picture of a restored city includes old people resting in the streets and children playing safely.** What would that kind of peace and safety look like in your neighborhood or your school? What's one thing you could do to help create it?

3. **Zechariah 9:9 describes a king who is "righteous and victorious, lowly and riding on a donkey."** Why do you think God chose a donkey instead of a warhorse? What does that tell us about the kind of kingdom Jesus came to build?

4. **Jesus quoted the shepherd passages from the prophets to describe himself.** What does it mean to you personally that God describes himself as a shepherd who goes looking for lost and scattered sheep?

5. **Zechariah promised that people from "all languages and nations" would seek God.** How does that promise connect to what's happening in the world today through the church? What role do you play in that story?

The humble king has been announced. The shepherd has promised to gather his flock. But Zechariah's final chapters will reveal something about this king that nobody was prepared to hear: before he reigns, he will be rejected. Before he saves, he will be struck down. And the price of his people's freedom will be paid in a currency that the whole world will recognize.

Turn the page.

7

THE ONE THEY PIERCED

One of the most famous moments in Arthur Conan Doyle's *Sherlock Holmes* stories comes in "The Final Problem," when Holmes confronts his greatest enemy. Professor Moriarty is the mastermind behind a vast criminal empire, and Holmes is the only person in the world who can stop him. But stopping Moriarty will cost Holmes everything.

Holmes knows this. He writes a farewell letter to Watson. He puts his affairs in order. And then he goes to Reichenbach Falls in Switzerland, where he meets Moriarty face to face. The two men struggle at the edge of the waterfall. And both of them go over.

Watson arrives too late. He finds the letter. He stares down into the churning water. And the world's greatest detective, the one person who could see what nobody else could see, is gone. Watson mourns. London mourns. Readers mourned so deeply when the story was published that some reportedly wore black armbands in the streets.

But here's the thing Doyle eventually revealed: Holmes wasn't dead. He had survived the fall. He had let the world believe he was gone because his work wasn't finished yet. And when he finally returned, everything changed.

A hero who willingly walks toward death. A world that mourns. And a return that changes everything. That's not just the shape of a detective story. It's the shape of what Zechariah describes in his final chapters. The king who rode into Jerusalem on a donkey, the shepherd who gathered his scattered flock, the Branch who was going to build God's temple—this same figure will be rejected by his own people, valued at the price of a slave, pierced, and struck down. And through that rejection and death, salvation will come to the world.

These are the most intensely messianic chapters in all of the Minor Prophets. After the Psalms, Zechariah is the most quoted Old Testament book in the Gospel accounts of Jesus' death. If you want to understand the cross, you need to read what comes next.

THIRTY PIECES OF SILVER

Zechariah 11 tells a story through a dramatic sign-act. God tells the prophet to play the role of a shepherd caring for a flock "marked for slaughter." The flock represents God's people, who have been abused and exploited by their own leaders. These leaders bought and sold the people for profit and then had the nerve to say, "Praise the Lord, I am rich!" They were supposed to protect the flock. Instead, they used the flock to enrich themselves.

The shepherd in the story (representing God) takes two staffs. He names one "Favor" and the other "Union." These represent God's covenant blessings and the unity of his people.

But the people reject the shepherd. They don't want his care. They don't want his leadership.

So the shepherd says: "If you think it best, give me my pay; but if not, keep it." And they pay him. Thirty pieces of silver.

That number matters enormously. In the law of Moses, thirty pieces of silver was the price paid for a slave who had been accidentally killed. It was the lowest value you could place on a human life. By paying the shepherd thirty pieces of silver, the people were saying, "That's all you're worth to us. The price of a slave."

God's response is biting: "Throw it to the potter, the handsome price at which they valued me!" The money is flung contemptuously into the temple.

Then the shepherd breaks both staffs. "Favor" is snapped, meaning God's protective covenant is revoked. "Union" is snapped, meaning the people are divided. Rejection of God leads to the loss of both his blessing and the community's unity.

Five hundred years later, a man named Judas walked into the chambers of the chief priests and asked, "What are you willing to give me if I deliver him over to you?" They counted out thirty pieces of silver. After the betrayal, when guilt overwhelmed him, Judas threw the money into the temple and went out and hanged himself. The priests used the blood money to buy a potter's field.

Matthew, writing his Gospel, looked at that scene and recognized it immediately: this was Zechariah's prophecy, playing out in real time. The Good Shepherd had come in person, and his own people valued him at the price of a slave.

THE ONE THEY HAVE PIERCED

Chapter 12 shifts to a future battle. The nations gather against Jerusalem, but God intervenes. He makes Jerusalem like an immovable rock that injures everyone who tries to move it. He protects his people and empowers them for victory. On that day, even the weakest person in Jerusalem will be like King David, and the house of David will be like God himself leading his people.

But then, in the aftermath of this great deliverance, something unexpected happens. God pours out "a spirit of grace and supplication," and the people look at what they've done: "They will look on me, the one they have pierced, and they will mourn for him as one mourns for an only child, and grieve bitterly for him as one grieves for a firstborn son."

Read that carefully. God says "me, the one they have pierced," and then shifts to "mourn for him." The people have pierced God and a closely connected person at the same time. The mourning that follows is deep, personal, and agonizing, the kind of grief you feel when you lose your only child or your firstborn son.

Who is this pierced figure? In the larger context of Zechariah, the answer is the same person who has been building throughout the book: the Branch, the priest-king, the shepherd, the king on the donkey. The Messiah.

The Gospel of John describes the moment after Jesus died on the cross: "One of the soldiers pierced Jesus' side with a spear, bringing a sudden flow of blood and water." Then John adds, quoting Zechariah directly: "These things happened so that the scripture would be fulfilled: 'They will look on the one they have pierced.'"

What follows the piercing in Zechariah is not rage or revenge. It's mourning. The people realize what they've done, and they weep. The grief spreads through every family, every clan, across the entire land. This isn't punishment. It's repentance. The piercing of God's chosen one opens the people's eyes to what they've been doing all along, and their hearts break.

STRIKE THE SHEPHERD

Chapter 13 continues the sequence. After the piercing and the mourning comes cleansing: "On that day a fountain will be opened to the house of David and the inhabitants of Jerusalem, to cleanse them from sin and uncleanness."

A fountain. Not a trickle, not a basin that has to be refilled, but a fountain, an abundant, ongoing, never-ending supply of cleansing. The death of the pierced one opens a permanent source of forgiveness.

Then comes one of the most sobering verses in the entire Old Testament, spoken by God himself: "Awake, sword, against my shepherd, against the man who is close to me! Strike the shepherd, and the sheep will be scattered."

God is commanding that his own shepherd, the man closest to him, be struck down. This isn't an accident. It isn't an enemy's scheme that God failed to prevent. It is God's own plan. The shepherd must be struck so that something new can emerge from the scattering.

On the night before his crucifixion, Jesus gathered his disciples for a final meal. He knew what was coming. And he quoted this exact verse to them: "You will all fall away, for it is written: 'I will strike the shepherd, and the sheep will be scattered.'"

The disciples didn't fully understand. They would soon. Within hours, Jesus would be arrested, and every one of them would run. The shepherd was struck, and the sheep scattered, exactly as Zechariah had written five centuries earlier.

But the scattering isn't the end. Zechariah says that after the shepherd is struck, a remnant will pass through fire and be refined like silver and gold. And then comes the covenant promise that runs through the entire Bible: "They will call on my name and I will answer them. I will say, 'They are my people,' and they will say, 'The LORD is our God.'"

The death of the shepherd doesn't destroy the flock. It refines it. The striking of the king doesn't end the kingdom. It establishes it.

THE LORD WILL BE KING

The final chapter of Zechariah pulls back to the widest possible lens. After the rejection, the piercing, the striking of the shepherd, and the refining of the remnant, God himself arrives.

He stands on the Mount of Olives, and the mountain splits in two, creating a valley through which his people can escape their enemies. Living water flows out from Jerusalem in every direction, in summer and in winter, never drying up. Darkness gives way to a unique kind of light, a day known only to God.

And then the climax of the entire book: "The LORD will be king over the whole earth. On that day there will be one LORD, and his name the only name."

Everything Zechariah has been building toward arrives here. The God who sent horsemen to patrol the earth in chapter 1, who cleansed his priest in chapter 3, who promised a king on a donkey in chapter 9, who allowed his shepherd to be struck in chapter 13—that God now reigns without rival over the whole earth.

The nations that once attacked Jerusalem will come to worship there. The Festival of Tabernacles, the great celebration of God's faithfulness, will include people from every nation. And holiness will spread from the temple outward until it covers everything. The words "HOLY TO THE LORD," once engraved only on the high priest's turban, will be written on the bells of horses and the cooking pots in every kitchen. The ordinary will become sacred. The common will become holy. Every square inch of creation will belong to God.

The book of Revelation takes these images and develops them into its final vision of a new heaven and new earth, where there is no more temple because God himself is the temple, where living water flows from his throne, and where there is no more night because his glory provides all the light anyone will ever need.

Zechariah saw it coming. Five hundred years before the cross, he described the cost. And he saw what lay on the other side of the cost: a kingdom that fills the earth, a fountain that never runs dry, and a God who reigns forever.

WHAT THIS MEANS FOR US

First, the cross was not an accident. Zechariah makes it clear that the striking of the shepherd was God's own plan. Jesus was not a victim of circumstances. His death was the most deliberate, intentional act in the history of the world, planned before the foundation of time and prophesied centuries in advance.

When you look at the cross, you're looking at something God designed to save you.

Second, rejection doesn't determine your value. The shepherd was valued at thirty pieces of silver, the price of a slave. But the value the world placed on him had nothing to do with his actual worth. If you've ever felt undervalued, overlooked, or dismissed by the people around you, remember: the most valuable person who ever lived was sold for pocket change. The world's assessment is not God's assessment.

Third, grief over sin is the doorway to healing. When the people in Zechariah's vision looked on the one they had pierced, they didn't get defensive or make excuses. They mourned. And that mourning opened the fountain of cleansing. Repentance isn't something to be afraid of. It's the path to the fountain. The tears are what carry you there.

Fourth, God's kingdom is coming and nothing can stop it. Zechariah 14 is the most confident chapter in the Minor Prophets. After all the rejection, all the suffering, all the scattering, God will be king over the whole earth. Every nation will worship him. Every cooking pot will be holy. The story doesn't end with a cross. It ends with a crown.

TALKING POINTS

1. **Zechariah's shepherd was paid thirty pieces of silver, the price of a slave. Five hundred years later, Judas betrayed Jesus for the same amount.** What does it tell you about God that he built these details into the story centuries in advance?

2. **Zechariah 12:10 says the people will "look on the one they have pierced" and mourn.** Why do you think seeing

what they had done led to mourning rather than anger or denial? What does genuine repentance look like?

3. Jesus quoted Zechariah 13:7 the night before he died: "Strike the shepherd, and the sheep will be scattered." Why do you think he chose that moment to quote those words? What was he trying to prepare his disciples for?

4. Zechariah 13:1 describes "a fountain opened to cleanse from sin." How is this image different from a one-time washing? What does it mean that forgiveness is described as a fountain rather than a bucket?

5. Zechariah's final vision includes "HOLY TO THE LORD" written on cooking pots and horse bells. What does it mean for ordinary, everyday things to be holy? What would it look like if you treated your everyday life as something sacred to God?

Zechariah's visions are finished. The night dreams, the humble king, the struck shepherd, the reigning God, it all points in one direction. But there's one more voice to hear before the Old Testament falls silent. One more prophet with one final message for a people who have grown tired of waiting and have started to wonder if any of it is worth the effort.

Turn the page.

8

THE LAST VOICE BEFORE THE DAWN

Have you ever given someone a gift that you didn't really put any thought into? Maybe it was a birthday party you didn't want to go to, and you grabbed something from the clearance bin on the way there. Or maybe it was a family gift exchange where you wrapped up something you'd found lying around the house, something you were basically going to throw away anyway. You showed up. You handed it over. You technically did what was expected.

But everyone knew. The person opening it knew. You knew. There's a difference between giving someone your best and giving someone your leftovers, and it's almost impossible to hide which one you're doing.

Now imagine that the person you were giving leftovers to was God.

That's the book of Malachi. It's a book about a nation that was still going through the motions of worship but had stopped meaning any of it. They brought sacrifices to the temple, but they brought the worst animals they had. They said the right words, but their hearts were somewhere else. They showed up, but they didn't care. And God, through his prophet, called them out on every single bit of it.

Malachi is the last prophetic voice in the Old Testament. After him, there would be roughly four hundred years of silence before an angel appeared to a priest named Zechariah (a different Zechariah) and the story of the New Testament began. What God chose to say through his final Old Testament prophet matters enormously, because these were his parting words to his people before the longest silence in biblical history.

And what he said, first and last, was this: "I have loved you."

A TIRED NATION

To understand Malachi, you need to feel the mood of his time. The temple had been rebuilt decades earlier, thanks to the work of Haggai, Zechariah, and the faithful remnant. The worship services were running. The priests were serving. On the surface, everything looked functional.

But the spark was gone. The great hopes that Haggai and Zechariah had stirred up—that God was going to shake the heavens and earth, that a glorious new era was dawning—hadn't materialized. The nations hadn't come streaming to Jerusalem. The messianic king hadn't appeared. Judah was still a tiny province in the vast Persian Empire, paying taxes to a foreign ruler and watching nothing change.

Disappointment had curdled into cynicism. The people weren't openly rebelling against God. They were doing something almost worse: they were going through the motions while internally deciding that none of it mattered. They had become spiritually numb.

Malachi stepped into that numbness around 460–430 BC. His name means "my messenger," and he had one final message to deliver before the prophetic voice fell silent.

"I HAVE LOVED YOU"

The book opens with God making the most personal declaration imaginable: "I have loved you." And the people's response tells you everything about their spiritual condition: "How have you loved us?"

They weren't being philosophical. They were being bitter. They looked at their circumstances, their small struggling community, their unfulfilled hopes, and they genuinely couldn't see evidence that God loved them. Life was hard. The economy was shaky. The promised future hadn't arrived. If this was love, they wanted a receipt.

God's answer pointed back to history. He reminded them of Jacob and Esau, the twin brothers from Genesis. God had chosen Jacob and his descendants, the nation of Israel, while Edom, the descendants of Esau, had been judged and devastated. The contrast was visible for anyone who cared to look. Edom lay in ruins. Israel still stood. God's love wasn't a feeling. It was a fact, written into the very landscape of the ancient world.

But the people couldn't see it. When you've decided that nothing matters, evidence of love can be staring you in the face and you'll still miss it.

GIVING GOD THE LEFTOVERS

The second disputation is where Malachi's message gets uncomfortably specific. God turns to the priests and says, "A son honors his father, and a servant his master. If I am a father, where is the honor due me? If I am a master, where is the respect due me?"

The priests respond with the question that runs like a refrain through the entire book: "How have we shown contempt for your name?"

God's answer: look at what you're putting on my altar. The law required that sacrificial animals be healthy and without defect. The whole point was that you were giving God your best, not your leftovers. But the priests had been accepting blind animals, lame animals, diseased animals. The animals nobody else wanted. The ones the farmers were happy to get rid of.

Then God delivers one of the sharpest lines in the Old Testament: "Try offering them to your governor! Would he be pleased with you? Would he accept you?"

In other words: you wouldn't dare give your Persian governor a sick, limping animal as a gift. You know he'd be insulted. But you bring those same animals to the God of the universe and expect him to be grateful?

Then comes a line so startling that it stops you in your tracks: "Oh, that one of you would shut the temple doors, so that you would not light useless fires on my altar! I am not pleased with you, and I will accept no offering from your hands."

God would rather have the temple doors locked and the fires put out than continue receiving worship that means nothing. Empty ritual isn't just unhelpful. It's offensive. God doesn't want your leftovers. He doesn't want your going-through-the-motions. He would rather have nothing at all than have a lie dressed up as devotion.

BROKEN PROMISES

The middle section of Malachi addresses two painful topics: faithless worship and faithless relationships.

The priests had corrupted their calling. They were supposed to be teachers of God's law, men whose "lips should preserve knowledge." Instead, they had turned from the path, caused others to stumble, and violated the covenant God had made with the tribe of Levi. The spiritual leaders had become spiritual liabilities.

Then Malachi turned to the community at large and addressed something that was tearing families apart: Jewish men were divorcing their wives to marry women from surrounding nations who worshiped other gods. The marriages weren't just personal failures. They were acts of spiritual treason, because they brought the worship of foreign gods into Israelite homes and compromised the faith of the next generation.

God's response was direct: "I hate divorce." Not because he wanted to trap people in misery, but because marriage was supposed to be a covenant, a binding promise. And a nation that couldn't keep its promises to each other was unlikely to keep its promises to God. The faithlessness in their marriages reflected the faithlessness in their worship. Both were symptoms of the same disease: a refusal to take commitments seriously.

"WILL A MAN ROB GOD?"

Perhaps the most famous passage in Malachi comes next. God says, "Return to me, and I will return to you." The people ask, "How are we to return?"

God's answer is surprisingly concrete: "Will a mere mortal rob God? Yet you rob me. In tithes and offerings."

The people had stopped bringing their full tithes to the temple. After the Persian government stopped funding the temple, the entire financial burden fell on the community. And the community had decided it couldn't afford it. They were giving less, cutting corners, holding back.

Then God does something he almost never does in the Bible. He issues a direct challenge: "Bring the whole tithe into the storehouse, that there may be food in my house. Test me in this, and see if I will not throw open the floodgates of heaven and pour out so much blessing that there will not be room enough to store it."

Test me. Those are extraordinary words from a God who usually says, "Do not put the Lord your God to the test." But here, on this one point, God invites the challenge. He says, in effect: "You think generosity will leave you worse off? Try it. Give me your best and see what happens."

This isn't a promise that giving money to God will make you rich. It's a promise that when God's people put him first, he doesn't leave them empty-handed. The point isn't the money. The point is trust. The people had been holding back because they didn't believe God would take care of them. God was asking them to act on faith and watch him respond.

"WHAT'S THE POINT?"

The final disputation strikes at the deepest level of the people's cynicism. God says their words have been "arrogant" against him. They ask, "What have we said?"

And God quotes back to them the attitude that had been poisoning the whole community: "It is futile to serve God. What do we gain by carrying out his requirements? The arrogant are blessed. Evildoers prosper. Those who challenge God get away with it."

That's the heart of their problem. Not idolatry. Not open rebellion. Just a quiet, corrosive conviction that being faithful to God is a waste of time. The people who cut corners get ahead. The people who cheat prosper. The people who ignore God seem to do just fine. So why bother?

If you've ever looked around your school, your neighborhood, or your world and thought the same thing, you understand exactly where these people were. Why be honest when liars seem to win? Why be kind when the mean kids are popular? Why follow God's rules when breaking them seems to have no consequences?

Malachi doesn't dismiss the question. But he does answer it.

THE SCROLL AND THE SUN

In the middle of all the cynicism, something quiet and beautiful happens. "Then those who feared the LORD talked with each other, and the LORD listened and heard. A scroll of remembrance was written in his presence concerning those who feared the LORD and honored his name."

Not everyone had given up. There was a faithful remnant, people who still took God seriously, who still talked about him with each other, who still lived as though he mattered. And God noticed. He didn't just notice. He wrote their names down. He kept a record. Their faithfulness was not invisible to him, even if it was invisible to the world.

"They will be mine," says the Lord, "in the day when I make up my treasured possession. I will spare them, just as a father has compassion and spares his son who serves him."

Then Malachi lifts his eyes to the future. A day is coming, he says, when everything will be set right. The arrogant and the evildoers will burn like stubble in a furnace. Nothing they built will survive. But for those who fear God's name, "the sun of righteousness will rise, with healing in its wings. You will go out and frolic like well-fed calves."

That image is extraordinary. After all the darkness of the book, after the cynicism and the leftovers and the broken promises, Malachi ends with sunrise. Not a scorching, punishing sun but a healing one. A sun with wings, like a great bird sheltering its young. And God's people, so long burdened and discouraged, will run and leap with the joy of calves released from a stall into an open field.

THE LAST WORDS

The very last paragraph of the Old Testament looks backward and forward at the same time. "Remember the law of my servant Moses," God says. Hold on to the foundation. Don't forget where you came from.

Then: "See, I will send the prophet Elijah to you before that great and dreadful day of the LORD comes. He will turn the hearts of the parents to their children, and the hearts of the children to their parents."

Moses and Elijah. Law and prophecy. The two pillars of the Old Testament, mentioned in the last breath before the silence.

Centuries later, on a mountain in Galilee, Jesus stood shining with glory, and two figures appeared beside him: Moses and Elijah. The disciples watched in awe as the law and the prophets, the very things Malachi had pointed to in his closing words, stood in the presence of the one they had always been pointing toward.

And the Elijah figure? Jesus said John the Baptist fulfilled that role. He came in the spirit and power of Elijah, turning hearts, preparing the way, calling people to repentance before the Lord arrived.

Malachi was the last voice. But he wasn't the last word. The silence that followed his prophecy wasn't the silence of abandonment. It was the silence of anticipation. Like the hush in a theater just before the curtain rises. Like the stillness of the world in the hour before dawn.

The sun of righteousness was coming. And when he arrived, he would have healing in his wings.

WHAT THIS MEANS FOR US

First, God's love is a fact, not a feeling. The people in Malachi's day couldn't feel God's love, so they concluded it wasn't real. But love isn't always visible in the moment. Sometimes you only see it when you look back. God's love for his people was woven into their entire history, and it hadn't stopped just because they couldn't feel it that Tuesday afternoon.

Second, God wants your best, not your leftovers. Whatever you give to God—whether it's your time, your energy, your attention, or your resources—give him the real thing, not the scraps you have left after everything else gets your best.

The question Malachi asks is still the right one: Would you offer this to someone you actually respected?

Third, faithfulness is never invisible to God. The world may not notice when you do the right thing. The cynics may mock you for it. But God keeps a scroll. He sees. He remembers. And the day is coming when the difference between the faithful and the faithless will be unmistakably clear.

Fourth, the story isn't over. Malachi ends the Old Testament, but he ends it looking forward. The sun is about to rise. Elijah is about to come. The silence between the Testaments isn't emptiness. It's the deep breath before the greatest story ever told begins in a stable in Bethlehem.

TALKING POINTS

1. **The people asked God, "How have you loved us?"** Have you ever felt that way, like God's love was hard to see? What helped you recognize it, or what would help you look for it?

2. **God said he would rather have the temple doors shut than receive meaningless worship.** What does "going through the motions" look like in your own faith? How can you tell the difference between genuine worship and just showing up?

3. **God challenged the people to "test him" with their tithes.** Why do you think God issued this challenge? What does it tell us about the relationship between generosity and trust?

4. **The people said, "It is futile to serve God."** Have you ever felt like doing the right thing doesn't matter because people who don't seem to do just fine? How does Malachi's answer, the scroll of remembrance and the coming day, change that feeling?

5. Malachi ends with the promise of Elijah and "the sun of righteousness rising with healing in its wings." What does that image mean to you? How does it feel to know that the Old Testament ends not with a period but with a promise?

The prophets have spoken. From Nahum's thundering announcement of Nineveh's fall to Malachi's quiet promise of a rising sun, the last six voices of the Old Testament have carried a single message through centuries of war, exile, rebuilding, and waiting: God is faithful. He judges because he is just. He restores because he is merciful. He refines because he is making something new.

And now the silence begins. Four hundred years will pass before a priest burns incense in the temple and an angel appears at his side. Four hundred years before a young woman in Nazareth hears the words, "You will conceive and give birth to a son." Four hundred years before shepherds hear singing in a midnight sky and wise men follow a star to a stable.

But the silence is not empty. It is full of promise. Because the last word of the Old Testament prophets is not judgment. It is not warning. It is not rebuke.

It is sunrise.

www.ingramcontent.com/pod-product-compliance
Lightning Source LLC
Chambersburg PA
CBHW051004050726
47592CB00007B/2698